Advance Praise for *If We Still Lived Where I Was Born*

In this collection, Giura skillfully weaves between the particular place and time of her youth to present day, eventually making her way back to her parents' ancestral villages in Italy. From a Sunday meal that becomes a holy experience to Aunt Rose *combing the ocean out of [her] hair*, Giura's poems are empathetic, evocatively drawn portraits. A wise and captivating collection.

JENNIFER ROMANELLO, contributor, *And There Were Red Geraniums Everywhere: Women's voices of the Italian diaspora in North America*

If I had to use only one word to describe this collection, it would be grace. It's grace that allows Giura to write the past with wisdom, forgiveness, and playfulness, masterfully leading us through the front door of her childhood home, into the bakery where her parents toiled and out the back door to love and heartbreak, connection and healing. Sharp and delicate like her mother's *good crystal . . . filled with burgundy wine,* these poems will stay with you long after the last sip.

JULIA PAUL, *Table With Burning Candle, Staring Down the Tracks* and *Shook*

VIA Folios 188

Also by the Author

What My Father Taught Me

Celibate: A Memoir

If We Still Lived
Where I Was Born

Published by Bordighera Press, an imprint of the John D. Calandra Italian American Institute of Queens College, The City University of New York.

25 West 43rd Street, 17th Floor, New York, NY 10036

Library of Congress Control Number: 2025942733

The cover photo is Verrazano Bridge at Sunset, New York, USA by Stef Ko, | Dreamstime.com.

© 2025, Maria Giura

VIA Folios 188
ISBN 978-1-59954-243-0

IF WE STILL LIVED WHERE I WAS BORN

Maria Giura

BORDIGHERA PRESS

Table of Contents

III.

People's faces change when they begin to say,
"I once went back to . . ."
Something is happening to them, some rich realization,
the thrill of retrieval . . . past and present in one.

ALASTAIR REID

For my mother and father, *always*.

Note to the Reader

A few years ago on a cool May day, I went on an excursion to a rock church in Basilicata Italy with about fifty fellow writers. Our guide used a single white light to show each of us to a seat in the dark. Then he cast the light on one wall at a time. We sighed in awe as biblical images sprung around us: apostles, archangels, virgin, Savior, and, on the back wall, episodes from creation—Adam raising his arms toward God as Eve emerges sumptuously from his rib, God portrayed as a long, delicate artist's hand, Eve holding out to Adam a suggestive fig.

It's called the Crypt of the Original Sin, but the frescoes felt alive, surrounded by joyful red flowers, which gave the 9th century unknown painter the nickname, The Flower Painter of Matera. Earlier that week, I had written a piece about how when I was little, I wrote on everything I could find, even on the walls in my Zia's apartment. I imagined my child self, maybe three or four years old, standing in front of that wall, exhilarated by the size of it—a whole wall with no margins. I believe it was the beginning of my creative impulse, the desire to grow something that was not there before. Like the cave drawings in the Crypt that weren't discovered until the 1960s, weren't restored for the public until 2005, the stories we tell, no matter how far back or how long they take to surface, are often stories of light and dark side by side.

I.

If We Still Lived Where I Was Born

we'd be in the apartment above the pastry shoppe
where downstairs my father made cannoli and eclairs and rum baba

and my mother made trays of butter cookies and rang up customers
and balanced the books.

The El would still be roaring passed our living room
shaking the couch in its wake.

Janine would still be the most popular kid in class
lugging home more Christmas gifts than any of us ever would,

still clinging to Grandma's leg when it was time for her
to go, coercing Julia

to ride her bike twenty-six blocks in the rain
to get her Nathan's.

Julie would still be testing limits--
eating a bottle of St. Joseph's orange aspirin,

promising our father's Italian ices to her entire class,
sticking our cat Gigi's head in the fish bowl to see if it would fit.

Nellie would still be that gleaming sliver
in my mother and father's eyes

another blue-eyed *capodosta* seven years into our future.
If we still lived where I was born,

I'd be holding out my arms for my mother
who used to sing "Close to You" to me

then left for work.
I'd still be writing on anything I could find:

walls, order forms, my mother's yearbook.
My father would still be climbing the stairs at 9 p.m.

smelling of almond paste and cigarettes,
brushing his five o' clock shadow against our tender skin.

My mother would still be at the stove,
giving everything she has away.

If we still lived where I was born,
we'd have those couple of hours a week

around the Formica table,
the four of them counting the cash after dinner,

putting it in a canvas bag for the bank
while my mother held me in her lap.

My mother and father would still be in their prime—
Isabella Rossellini and James Dean look-alikes.

They'd still be fighting,
they'd still be making us,
we'd still be together.

My Parents Long Ago

In this picture,
my mother and father
no more than eighteen and twenty-two
stand in the center
no space between them,
surrounded by family.

She's wearing a jumper dress
and he a tie and vest,
his head playfully tilted toward her
his arm so far around her shoulder,
it almost drapes her elbow.

She's standing straight,
head held model-high,
class ring on the hand she rests
on her grandmother
who sits in front of her.

Next to my parents, my grandparents—
my grandfather,
also an Anthony,
with the same vest and tilt
and my grandmother
looking into the camera
with a smile that grows inside her,
her parents *here,* in her house—

my great grandparents
who want to return to Sicily,
but for now, fold their hands on the table
like sweet school children.
Everyone else is smiling,
teeth like pearls in black and white,
my mother's aunt and brother-in-law,
a small niece and nephew.

Even Padre Pio,
the saint with the stigmata,
framed on the wall behind them
glows.

Five decades later,
my mother frames this picture
puts it on her desk
even though she and my father
divorced so many years before,
married other people.

I know it's a moment
that's locked forever,

but I want to climb inside
and turn the key.

First Bedroom

We had twin beds—
Julie and I—
pink and white gingham spreads
separated by a window
that overlooked the clothesline.

We had two hassocks
—one pink, one green—
a nightstand between our beds,
a crochet doll that fit over the tissue box.

On the wall, a framed poster of ballet slippers.
A thin, swirly carpet
and spiral staircase
that circled down to our older
sister Janine's bedroom.

Our bedroom nestled in between
the oldest and the youngest
like our place in the family,
though Julie six years older than me.

One night, I was not yet nine,
Papa appeared at our window
trying to get back in the house
after our mother had locked him out again.

Julie was sleeping soundly
even though I called her name

though maybe not loud enough,
afraid she wouldn't be able
to send him away. I didn't want to either,
but I knew our mother was right.

I pretended not to hear our father
as he fought to fit his calloused hand
through the metal gates
he'd installed just a few weeks earlier,
because a burglar had made his way inside.
He knocked on the window, called
Belle figlie, belle figlie,
Beautiful daughters,
beautiful daughters.

I sat up stiff against my headboard
so he wouldn't see me,
looked sideways at Julie's bed
called her name again but nothing.

I let our father walk away
knowing he had nowhere to go,
heard the crunch of leaves beneath his feet,
the small clatter of clothespins in the wind.

Sicily in June

This January, grey and endless,
I long for the trip to Sicily
on the calendar for June,
my mother, sisters and I
together for the first time
in the place she was born.

We will stay at a villa in Taormina
overlooking coves and piazzas,
churches and Greek theatre.
From there we will go south to Mount Etna
and north to Messina
to see the clock
whose statues
move like life-sized toys.

Then on to San Pier Niceto where our mom
lived her first eight years.
She once told me that
no one ever talked to her—
her parents and middle sister working
the farm from sunrise to sunset,
her oldest sister busy with all the housework
then sneaking out for a visit with friends.
My mother said it was just her and the cat,
the bowl of milk.

We will see the house where
that small blue-eyed girl lived

who gave birth to four blue-eyed daughters.
We will go to Tindari
overlooking the Tyrrhenian
with its tongue of sand
and pilgrimage to the Byzantine Madonna
who protected a ship from storm
then insisted she'd remain on shore.

We will sip prosecco and caffè,
eat bowls of fresh pasta,
lick gelato while we walk.
We'll go in and out of sun
looking for treasures we will find.

My mother will tell us
she doesn't remember much as we climb the hill
to campagna where my grandparents and aunt
carried wheat on their heads,
and pulled down prickly pears from trees,
where the three sisters shared one doll,
and found orange and walnuts
in their shoes on Christmas.

We will spend time the five of us,
four thousand miles
from this relentless January,
in country that looks like a painting,

turquoise and limestone and sky
where the hungry girl who no one talked to
will be surrounded by three seas and
daughters whose favorite pastime is to chew her ear.

Mass in Rochester

During a visit to my sister's,
my father walks me to the end of her block
where Northfield meets Seneca
and watches until I disappear

into St. Margaret Mary's
where votives burn.
I pray for him
to the trinity of love,
to a Son who raises the dead.

A God who knows why
he's always wrestled authority,
why he was so angry with women,
why he grows frustrated watching
me play with my niece,
"But that baby, she won't let you go."

Mass has always felt like home to me.
So has my father,
a baker,
a workaholic who was never home,
who never listened,
who, when I retrace my steps
after Mass,
is waiting for me on the corner of Northfield,
bread in his hand.

Call the Midwife

On *Call the Midwife*,
Sister Monica Joan asks Mrs. Turner, a former nun,
which side is better.
"Neither and both.
We don't choose. We're chosen."
I want to ask my mother if she caught that,
does she understand?
She keeps saying she hopes
Trixie and Reggie meet someone,
that Nurse Crane, the self-proclaimed spinster, meets someone.
When I remind her she's content, she says, "She came alive
when she met that man in her Spanish class, but he's married.
Maybe she and the sergeant one day."

Many years ago, we ran into an acquaintance at the mall
who told us she'd just adopted a child,
joy puffing her cheeks.
"That's wonderful," my mother said, and then,
"Maybe now you'll meet someone."
I wanted to descend into a dot down the escalator.
Another time she told me one of her cousins never married;
she said it as if she had cancer.

This mother who had to divorce my father after seventeen years,
whose second husband died after only fourteen,
this mother who never wanted anything more than a happy family,
who dreamed of her own Mr. North from the radio show
who spoke to Mrs. North as his equal, who *cherished* her.

This mother who's always given more than she's taken,
who still has no idea what I'm thinking:
does she see my *life as incomplete, ill- fated?*
I have the urge to ask, but I don't think I will.
Maybe, finally, after all these years,
I can be the daughter who doesn't need to know,
the daughter who understands.

Driving North on 287

Driving north on 287
this gloomy, December morning,
I think of Tyler Clementi.
A moment later, an exit for Rutgers.

Maybe because I have a student
who's different than his classmates,
who has lots of friends who are girls
but no girlfriend yet.

Maybe because I've never liked
the George Washington Bridge,
with its eight lanes and thick towers,
its strange, complicated exits.

Maybe because I'd read
he had just come out,
that it was his first time
when his roommate taped him.

I wish I could have spoken to him
for just a little while
taken his face into my hands,
tried to convince him he's eternally loved.

This sensitive, accomplished soul
who, eight days from now,
would have turned thirty,
was so afraid, so ashamed,

he plunged 200 feet
rather than face his parents,
rather than face this world.

Still Matters

for Bob

I believe the trees and morning glories he planted are still breathing
oxygen,
his gardening tools still warm in my mother's hands.
I believe the paint brushes he left in the box on the top shelf in the
garage still give color,
the nuts and bolts stored in take-out soup containers still fixing
what's broken.
I believe his jumper cables in my trunk are still starting what needs
to be started,
his shovels still digging us out,
the copper-colored blanket his mother knitted still giving warmth.
I believe the marlin he caught that hung in the laundry room is still
receiving oohs and aahs,
the Follies he kept on tape still dancing.
I believe the pictures his sister painted, the music his nephew made,
still filling a room.
I believe his coffee table that opens up for storage still holding what
matters,
the cherry-wood desk he worked at late at night still serving a
purpose,
the leftover wood from the deck he built still holding us up.
I believe the fourteen-years-worth of home videos he took still live
inside their cases,
his suits my mother gave to goodwill still getting the job done,
the watches she gave his sons and grandsons still clocking time.
I believe that Herbal Life and the daily tablespoon of cod liver oil
kept him healthy
until they didn't,

the boxes of office supplies and reams of stationery with his slogan
"We mark it sold" his way
of trying to go on forever.
I believe he believed in the power of positive thinking that he kept
on the shelf
but that eluded him near the end.
I believe that even though he's gone, everything he leaves behind
still matters.
I believe I will find it all when I need it most.

St. Mary's of the Lake

"Perched on our shoulders, / the dead ride with us,
teetering like pyramids of water skiers, forming / enormous
wings."--Barbara Crooker

I.

The first night
of a residency where I know no one
I go down to the lake
wound up from the long drive,
watch the sun set on the Adirondacks.
It's Sunday night, weekenders gone,
a calm begins to settle. A few yards away,
a father lights a fire,
a child tubes, a mother
shouts, "Stay close to the pier."
I feel, not lonely, but aware of my aloneness
as I try to massage the migraine away,
try to slow down like the lake
lulling against its rocks,
when I think of my stepfather
whose legs were more sea than land,
who tried to teach me to take my time,
enjoy life more.

II.

I parallel play with poets
who write in their rooms with doors open
or gather together on porches facing the lake.
I pray, I write, I idle and read
I try writing exercises I'd never try at home,

picking twenty words randomly
and writing from them
which leads to this.
I go down to the lake again
this time to kayak with new friends
who instruct me to hold the paddle lightly,
to relax my grip,
the opposite of what I'd thought.
The next day strolling Beach Street
where the lake begins
and the steamboats await their passengers,
I spot my stepfather on his sailboat
one foot on deck, one on the bow
smiling at me,
tipping his cap.

Uncle Mimi

You came to me in a dream one early morning
on the Ionian coast,
not far from where you were born.

Tall and young,
posing at a family gathering.
Uncle Mimi, it's been so long
then you were gone.

When I woke, I thought of you in your Italian suits
swirling macadamia nuts in your palm
like an aristocrat,
how you'd wanted my cousin—your youngest—and me
to take ballroom dance lessons on Saturday afternoons,
but I said no, afraid I'd miss out on birthday parties.

I thought of how I was always afraid my elbows
would land on your and Aunt Anna's
dinner table where they didn't belong,
and how you didn't want me to go into teaching,
though I wound up in education anyway.

I thought about the way you helped get me into
Catholic high school half way through freshman year
and how you tried to teach me mind over matter
by tickling me, then expecting me not to laugh.

I thought about how you showed up at our door
with a dozen glazed donuts every Sunday morning,

and how you loved to twirl Aunt Anna
and Aunt Rose and my mother
on the dance floor,
you the only
husband left until my mother remarried.

I think of your baby photo
hanging in your home—
you naked, bottom up,
on a fur rug,
how you have always liked the
finer things in life, Uncle Mimi.

I think about how, if you had lived
past sixty, you wouldn't have agreed
with the choices I've made,
but how you would've—
all these years later—
still loved me like a daughter.

I Come from a Long Line of Workers

My paternal grandfather, a blacksmith in Basilicata,
cooking and shaping iron
into horseshoes and handrails,
banisters and tools,
my father and uncle his apprentices
while my grandmother cooked and cleaned
and scrubbed the laundry
she carried back and forth from the fountain
in the center of town.

My maternal grandparents, farmers in Sicily,
climbing the mountain
tending the animals, growing the food
my grandfather would cart hours away to sell in Messina.
My Aunt Anna working with them
every day sunrise to sunset,
while Aunt Rose stayed behind
with all the housework
and to watch my mother, the baby,

who came here at eight with her family
who was cooking dinner by eleven,
my mother who'd grow up to have multiple careers—
a bank and insurance company while still in high school,
the pastry shoppe where she met my father
then onto the next one they'd buy together,
working side by side for the next fifteen years

their hands in everything:
ovens, freezers, showcases,
cookies and pastries,
wedding cakes as high as dreams.

My father who came here at eighteen
who'd learn hundreds of recipes by heart
churning them out week after week
holiday after holiday
never taking a day off.

My mother whose work was never done,
up early and late to take care of the house,
of us.

After the divorce,
she bought a card store with a friend and her husband—
short lived since my mother's vision
was fine chocolates and gifts
and his, comic books and penny candies.
After this, she helped a little, blond boy, Patrick,
who went into the hospital for tonsilitis and
came out paralyzed,
who needed round-the-clock volunteers
to move his limbs.
Back in school for physical therapy,
she survived Chemistry and Gross Anatomy
among younger students,
received her Bachelor's and Master's
worked in a Catholic hospital she loved,
where she helped heal stroke patients,
and accident victims,
the elderly and injured.
Then onto a school
for children with developmental disabilities
where she became director,

and later a stint teaching college.

I come from a long line of workers

my father toiling since fifth grade
fueled by the reward of hard work,
not being poor like during the war,
proud when he'd made deliveries
to his father's wealthy customers
who had intercoms at their door,
proud when my grandfather called him *Maestro Tony.*
My father who stood fourteen-hour days
at the huge butcher block counter
rolling out dough, lifting canisters of lard,
lugging sacks of sugar as heavy as bodies,
who didn't sit until he made deliveries
to Gargiulio's, Rex Manor, El Caribe.
My father with no diploma or degree
adding an addition to the bakery
for ices, soft serve ice cream, cremolata.
My father who bought other businesses
after he sold the pastry shoppe to my uncle:
a caffe, a Russian restaurant, a Scandinavian bakery.

All these years later,
both my parents still working,
even though retired for years.
My mother still keeping a beautiful home
weeding the garden,
making delicious dinners
crocheting forty hours a week for charity,
my mother who won't watch TV
without a skein of yarn,
a blanket blooming in her lap.
My father still managing the one building he's kept
collecting the rents, planting his tomatoes

visiting friends who have grown lonely,
paying for their espressos
and just the other day,
for the first time in twenty-five years,
making my sisters and me cheesecakes
as creamy and airy as when we were kids.

I come from a long line of workers
both parents still teaching me
how to make something that wasn't there before,
how to give it all away.

Aydan

Your mother's white blond hair,
and great grandfather's light blue eyes,
little rubber bands of fat
at neck and elbows, knees and thighs,
and two tiny bottom teeth
when you smile and laugh.

Your *Dada* babble,
sounds aching to be words,
and your smell
of sweet morning dew.

From your stroller you lean over,
eye level with puppies
and statues of the Blessed Mother,
studying them, the world,
then slip into glorious sleep.

Later,
we pass you around the table
like a meal,
Or call out your name.
Sometimes you stare into trees, clouds, faces
at worlds I've forgotten,
heaven, here, now.

I want to be where you are, little boy,
where you go when you leave a room--
I sit holding you,

gold in my lap,
my nose in your hair,
hungry for the Eden
you never left.

Sunday

Grandparents, aunts and uncles,
cousins, friends,
relatives from Italy and Argentina
crowding our dining room
with its glass ceiling and chandelier,
the bow-bay window that looked out
onto 12 Avenue
with its emerald squares of lawn.

The solid mahogany table,
with its trunk-like legs and two leaves,
blooming with conversation and laughter,
my mother's sauce and fresh pasta
steaming from the bone china
and the good crystal from the breakfront

filled with burgundy wine.

After dinner, sfingi and zeppole
dressed up on white doilies,
espresso served in doll-sized cups,
and Mario Lanza and Sergio Bruni
singing in our stereo.

(Or the day Mario Abbate
signed albums in our living room,
his Neapolitan tenor
pouring through the house.)

My mother's hair piled
on her head like a queen
as she served course after course
barely sitting to take a bite.
My sisters and I her charges
helping to clear dishes, entertain guests.
My father at the head,
in pastry-stained uniform,
regaling everyone with stories.

If I close my eyes, I am there,
can see the light coming in the window
like another guest,
can taste the love and song,
the thrill of being young.
If I close my eyes, I see those Sundays
were another Mass, another eucharist

—a glimpse of the banquet to come.

II.

La vita è bella

An hour into the movie,
Guido, played by Roberto Benigni,
tells his four-year-old, Giosuè,
that the concentration camp is a game,
the prize a tank.

As the German soldier spits orders,
Guido translates the rules,
"Don't cry. Don't ask for food.
Don't ask for your mother."
If you do, the soldiers will put a sign on your back
Jackass or I ate too many lollipops.
He moves his shoulders the exact way the soldier does,
sweats through his earnestness,
Giosuè buys it.

Outside the ovens,
the barbed wire.

Inside the dark theatre,
I cry beside a man I have no future with.
We know nothing about love.

The first part of the movie
Guido's passion for Dora so pure,
she says yes even though she's more beautiful
and graceful and serious than he.
Then the second half.
I'd never seen a movie so haunting.

Now, Ukrainian fathers wrenched
from wives and children,
mothers and babies crossing borders
they never planned
without their Guidos,
without the men, who only for love,
can make hatred seem a game.

Sister of Charity

She told me God only invites,
never forces—
the purpose of discernment
to draw closer,
to become *fire*.

I visited her for years,
sat across from her
in her small office
with the pull-out love seat
where she slept when she gave retreats
to men and women,
people in recovery, AIDS patients.

She wore shin length dresses
and tie-up shoes,
a silver necklace with Elizabeth's profile

--their founder, who had been happily married
with five children until she was twenty-nine,
when her husband died of tuberculosis,

who had adored their life
didn't want to lose him,
wear a widow's cap, become a nun,

who closed the gap for me,
made celibacy seem less strange.

Each month before I left,
Sister Erin offered a line of Scripture,
made me hunger for more.
When I didn't enter the Order,
she told me I needed to date,
that the man I thought I loved
didn't love me.

All those years, a God who hurt,
or at best withheld,
Sister Erin gently healed,
put me back together,
hugged me tight like a pile of leaves
afraid one would slip.

Surprise

Walked into the party wind-blown from the ocean,
baseball cap on, closest friends and family
yelling "Surprise!" which I greeted with enough
pleasured shock to throw them off.
After I showered and changed,
mixing with my guests,
chatting, laughing
swaying to R&B,
all of us wearing leis and drinking
wine coolers from giant cups,
the mild summer night a caress on our skin,
my sister's hydrangea plentiful in the air.

When I look back on that night, that birthday, that age,
a quarter century,
some of those friends no longer in my life
including Ted who was an unhappy architect
who wanted to move to Provence to cook
and asked me to drive on our dates,
who relied on me to do the breaking up.
So many people step in and out of our lives,
relationships meant to last only a span,
maybe for some goodness or lesson or pain.
The ones who remain, their stories
deepen into ours.
Those who'd spend a whole day
hosing down a backyard
and marinating meat,
taking you out on a boat.

Admissions

The day the Dean
told us they fired our Director,
locked him out,
my face turned to stone.
I think I said,
This is wrong.
How can you do this to someone?

How could they have not known
he wasn't a fit for our college,
for an administration that was Ivy League,
who wore Brooks Brothers,
who insisted we refer to the cafeteria as the dining hall
and the dorms, residence halls?

How could they have allowed him
to relocate six hours from home,
from Watertown? Expected him
to turn the tide of declining enrollment
in less than a year,
set him up for such failure?

I couldn't imagine the possibility
he'd done something egregious,
something they couldn't tell us—
this forty-something husband and father
being shown the door
while we, bright, shiny twenty-five-year-olds,
sat around a solid oak table

deciding who gets in, who stays out.

All I could see was the way
they often looked down
on Italian-American students
because of their New York accents,
because they stayed close to home,
the same students who made up
more than fifty percent of their enrollment,
who were their bread and butter,
the students who were the same ethnicity as me.

Arizona

That August evening,
my friend and I drove
from Flagstaff to Sedona
mesmerized by the profusion
of pine, the curve of road,
the reddening rock.

When we reached *Bella Terra,*
I ordered what I never do,
the filet mignon, tender, velvety,
and Laura, the Bolognese and chianti
which turned her face rose.

The following morning, we headed
for the Grand Canyon,
passed a field of black-eyed Susans so vast
like thousands of bright-haired children,
their faces to sun.

At the South Rim, I stepped out
onto a precipice finally letting go
of a man I'd been holding onto
for years,
how free I felt
in the midst of all that burnt-orange majesty.

Each day, we woke,
sat in our beds
drinking coffee

talking,
laughing,
staring at each other,
stunned by this state
neither of us had been to before.

Back in Sedona,
Laura stayed in to pray;
I went out,
sat criss-cross on sandstone,
watching the sunset,
buoyed by the vortex.

At the Chapel of the Holy Cross
we gazed on Jesus in the host,
on the cross.
For years it scared me—
a God who could let his own Son
be murdered? Now, I saw

the two as One,
their wide, cobalt sky behind Them,
their red rocks rising.

I forgot myself,
the prayer I'd clutched for years,
slipping from my hands
without my knowing.

In Praise of Silence

It used to terrify me
especially on three-day weekends.
Afraid God would speak,
that I would hear,
I'd drown Him out with plans, activity,
motion.

Now I go on week-long silent retreats—
take long walks on sand,
watch the Atlantic move like a caravan,
relish the peace of eating with others
not having to speak.

Now I ask for a seat
far away from the woman
talking nonstop on her cell,

miss the days when the only time
you could call
was when you got home.

Now I love the quiet
of late night and early morning
the clock and the wind chime,

love when the world seems asleep,
when it too seems to savor the silence,
when it might just be possible
to hear the *still small voice*.

If I Could Wrap Myself in a Color

If I could wrap myself in a color,
it'd be blue,
like the Ionian Sea
where you can see straight down to your toes.
Or richer, like the grotto of Capri
or the indigo the Atlantic becomes
when you swim into the deep.
Better yet, the magenta in Van Gogh's *Starry Night*,
the blue-black pre-dawn
in Hayden's "Those Winter Sundays,"
or the blue outside right now at 4:25 pm
on this 18th of December.
This is the blue—
sea,
painting,
poem,
night—
I'd throw around me to keep me warm.

Last Supper I

Beneath the tabernacle
in St. James Church,
a marble Last Supper.

Shocked faces,
flailing arms
reaching to touch Him
as if that will reverse fate,

except for Judas

and this disciple at Jesus's right
whom I can't look away from.

Long hair, soft face
leaning into love.

I'm not making it up;
I don't want to be a priest.
There's a girl
at Jesus' right hand,
and she knows.

Last Supper II

Beneath the tabernacle
in St. James Church,
a marble Last Supper.

Shocked faces,
flailing arms
reaching to touch Him
as if that will reverse fate,

except for Judas

and this disciple at Jesus' right
whose hair is long
and face soft,
who leans into love.

Staring into him
still young enough
to be feminine,
I finally understand
why he's the one Jesus loved.

It's Because

after Ross Gay's "A Small Needful Fact"

It's because George Floyd worked
security for a shelter,
made the homeless feel safe,
smiled at them, looked in their eyes,
called them by name,
the way he did the boys he mentored.

It's because he made music,
wrote songs about
Houston's Third Ward
where he grew up,
because he put lyrics in young men's minds,
might've helped them sprint
into a future, not a statistic.

It's because he wanted
a commercial driver's license
but dropped out, needed
that bouncer job at El Nuevo Rodeo
where he met the cop
who one day would murder him.

It's because his death brings Eric Garner back,
his open-hearted smile.
Killed six years earlier—
eight miles from where I live
where he planted trees—
his breath strangled

by the same kind of hands.

It's this that leads this white woman
to try and write about
these men, these fathers
whose final pleas reverberate,
these men whose lives she knows little about.

Faith Is

Faith is sitting
on the edge of your mother's bed—
her white hair fragile as tissue paper—
holding her forehead while she heaves,
praying it's not the virus.

Faith is taking her temperature,
believing the thermometer works.
It's bringing her ginger ale and decongestant
and later Tylenol and toast,
making some rice to ease her stomach,
hoping it will heal.

Faith is seeing her watch some TV,
proof she's starting to feel better.
Then letting her go back to bed,
trusting she'll wake again.

One day you will lose this mother,
the best person to happen to you.
One day you will have to let her go,
the way too many already have.

Faith is believing that this spring
outside our windows, and on our walks,
this spring we cannot touch—
is real.

Birthday 2020

Mid-August birthday usually bright, warm.
This year—rainy, sixty something degrees—

the remnants of Josephine,
tropical depression fizzled at sea.

The day before, sunny, eighty degrees,
filled with poetry, prayer,

dinner with favorite people
at an outdoor terrace

brimming with trellised-hibiscus
and waiters able to make us laugh
behind our masks.
Why then this sadness today—
the day I was born—

this sense of loss, anxiety,
the tears I cry in private, brief but real?

Is it the passing of time?
My expectations higher than I have right to?

Is it that there's no one person all my own?
(A choice I've embraced, mind you.)

Is this why I feel keenly separate,
this strange August day sitting

at Sunday Mass socially-distanced,
no sign of peace?

Rahner says God is our unsolved remainder
when our plans and experiences

don't balance out.
And Rumi, this being human a guest house,

that we should welcome every arrival,
even sorrow.

When I think of climate change

I'm scared the seasons will vanish.

I've never envied Florida or San Diego,
snow birds whisking off for six months of same.

It's the turn that always brings me hope,
the first sign of something new, again--
breath, bud, rose, leaf.

I'm afraid extreme is all we'll know,
no breezes anymore, no light wind for birds to sail.
I'm afraid the storms will continue to batter
making streets into oceans,
boats into life lines.

I'm afraid fire will continue to scorch
and tornados twist where they've never before.

I'm afraid hurricanes will come earlier and stay later,
nature swallowing more of the innocent.

I'm afraid of a world where the flip of a calendar
won't show a new day,
won't give us a chance to miss what's gone,

a world where we won't
have to pull the right wardrobe

from the back of the closet,
a world that no longer
clothes us in beauty.

I Used to Listen to
the Saddest Love Song

I used to listen to the saddest love song—
"I Can't Make You Love Me"—
especially in the months before breaking up
with my first real boyfriend.
"Why such a sad song?" he asked innocently,
when he heard it on my voicemail.
"I like it," I said, lying.
He wasn't my soul-mate, my forever,
the direction my life was supposed to go.
 "You Can't Make Me Love You"
would've been more accurate,
but I was grateful for this small mercy
as I tried preparing him and me,
but especially me,
for the long loneliness to come.

For Dave

The picture of health
in our early twenties—
blonde, green-eyed, tall and lean.

Three months ago
diagnosed with lung cancer,
though you never smoked.

We ran into each other
eight years ago
swimming in the Atlantic.
We hadn't seen each other
in close to twenty years.

Ocean glistened your skin
as I told you I was writing a book,
that whenever I thought of you,
it was fondly. As you told me

about your siblings,
that your son had his meets
at the university where I taught.

I remember how numb
I felt walking back to my towel—
the wave of what-ifs—
though I know we went the paths
we were supposed to.

Everywhere we went,
the air was clean:
Lambertville, New Hope,
High Point State Park,
all places I'd never been before.
The two of us on your motorcycle,
riding into light.

You—who took over a month
to kiss me, told me
I was worth waiting for—
now gone.

It's not so surprising
you died young—
the good sometimes do—
that your kids were your life
or that you provided well for them,
not surprising you moved to Monmouth County
like so many our age.

I hope we'll see each other again one day,
that I'll get to where you are,
where no one marries
or is given in marriage,

where all live like angels
and the air is clean,
where work can't harm a person,
and the only thing that matters
is how well he loved.

Encounter

for James

We ran into each other at the gym,
hadn't seen each other in sixteen years.
"Aren't you going to say hello?" he asked,
and I said "Wow" and "Wow" and *"Hello."*
He looked skinny, gaunt,
like a slice of himself,
like a ghost.
After the stunned hellos,
I walked outside where the light hurt,
and the late November leaves hung on.
What would have I said,
"How's your wife?" "Are you sick?"
I couldn't, didn't want to.
Whispered a prayer
whenever I thought of him.

In August
no birthday email from him,
even though I received one every year.
Now last night,
I learn he has weeks to live.
This man who used to bench 300
and order two entrees,
who told me I was the only woman
he wanted to marry.
This man who I thought would live to eighty,
and hoped I'd get to see one last time,
walk in sunlight together.

This morning,
the first day of spring—
the buds on the maple
like bright beads of blood—
I write him an email
I'm so sorry you're suffering,
I wish you the deepest peace.
I don't use the word dying,
but it's clear it's final,
that all those seasons ago,
when we were convinced
we'd be in each other's lives forever,
have come to this.

My Best Friend's Wedding

The movie ends the way it should—
good girl gets the guy,

not the girl who only wants him
because she can't have him,
who's willing to sell her soul
to keep him.

I cry tears that blotch my face
not because the good girl has won,
has married the guy,
but because this other girl
sits at their wedding alone
as all the couples dance,

until her dashing friend
who's flown from New York
to surprise her,
phones her from a few tables away.

He speaks of the lavender dress
she's wearing,
her fingers thrumming
the white linen table cloth,
the band suddenly playing,
"Say a Little Prayer…"

When she finds him,
he peels their phones away,

takes her hand, announces,
"There may not be sex or marriage,
but *by God*, there'll be dancing"
and twirls her into the night.

Making a Living

At fifteen, serving ziti and parmigiana
to the lunch crowd,
where the register flustered me,
and I'm sure I lost the owners money.
Then a page at the New Utrecht Branch,
shelving and checking out books for patrons,
getting first dibs on new books.
In the college Dean's Office,
filing disciplinary notices for classmates I never met,
whose names I memorized without trying.
Then, for a shopping circular,
laying out copy, writing promos
I didn't receive bylines for.
After college, an Admissions counselor
for my alma mater, where I learned
to speak in front of hundreds of people.
In between, covering the college for the local paper,
writing newsletters, brochures, poems,
any genre I could get my hands on.
Next, Career Placement,
helping students write resumes, meet alumni, get jobs,
the business professor who hired me advising,
Report on something
at every *department heads meeting*--
the best advice I ever received,
since I was one of only three women in the room
and, at twenty-seven, the youngest.
It was one of my favorite jobs,
making matches, meeting companies,

made me feel not just helpful but important.
After that, a PhD I pursued
because it got me to begin the memoir
I may have never written,
taught me to stay still at a desk
long enough to listen for the story.
Then teaching college writing for years.
More than fifty students a semester,
five papers each with three drafts—
bright, unprepared students
struggling with sentences.

It's always been administration I've preferred,
where I'm back again,
which feels natural,
gives me time to write.

It's always been writing I've come back to,
where I feel most at home, lost in time,
like maybe if I make it to heaven one day,
it'll be this I get to do for all eternity.

What Makes Me Happy

is this poem I didn't know I had.

To arrive at the solarium
with empty hands
except for what I saw on the road—

a stone church so charming
it could be on a manor,
a sign above the road,
Town-Wide Garage Sale,
a general store at the corner
of West Mendham.

Different ways of getting
to this quiet and green,
spring and red brick and English nuns,
whose vespers will float through the air
even if we don't hear them.

Across the way, each of us,
pen to paper, fingers to keys
praying the stories will find their way
through our cloud,
words rising from cool ground
as clear and true as tolling bell.

III.

Shame

Everything in kindergarten had been easy,
half-day. Pictures of primary colors,
and the colors they made together,
hung on tiled columns in our classroom.
We wore play clothes and sang,
practiced our letters, traced our hands.

First grade was big desks,
science, math, social studies,
crisscross ties at our necks.
I worried I wouldn't be able to do the work
that my mother would forget to pick me up
that I'd fail all the tests.

One morning, I felt my breakfast
start to rise up my insides,
asked Sister Ernestine
if I could be excused,
careful not to grip my stomach,
so she wouldn't know.

As soon as I closed the door,
I raced for the students' bathroom
but couldn't make it,
barged into the bathroom
marked TEACHERS, prayed no one
was there. Before I could get to the toilet,
tears and toast erupted.

Afterward, I stood on tippy toes,
threw water on my mouth,
gathered paper to wipe the floor,
cleaned up as best I could.
Less than a half hour later,
another teacher whispering something
in Sister's ear, and then "Stop everything,
put your pencils down,
which one of you children threw up
in the teacher's bathroom?"

I don't remember how long I stayed
silent, my head up,
so no one would suspect.
I just remember how ashamed I felt,
afraid everyone would find out
my inside didn't match my outside,
that I wasn't always the neat little girl,

like Leticia R. whose crisscross tie
never came loose,
whose long, smooth hair
fell like a black cascade down her back,

who looked like she never lied or got sick
or afraid, who didn't cling to the
the words at Communion like I did:
Protect us from all anxiety
as we wait in joyful hope.

Battatina

My favorite doll
had silky blond hair and big eyes,
pale plastic limbs and a soft middle
with a tiny record player in her back like a secret.

She came with records the size of *pignoli* cookies
and played songs like
batti le manine.

I'd spied her before she'd been given me,
a gift from Italy
left out on a shelf in the bookkeeping office
in a box like the kind they brought babies home in.

She was practically eye level,
so I couldn't help it,
snuck in to look at her
among the bills and counting machine,
keeping vigil until my birthday.

Afterward, I held her
as if she came from me,
as if I'd given birth,
fed her with a bottle whose milk tipped inside
when I brought it to her full pink lips,
pushed her in a navy-blue carriage
with the canopy raised
even when we were inside.

I played with her while my parents worked
while my sisters were at school,
as song poured from her back.
I carried her up and down
the length of the bakery.

On one end, my mother in her apron and high hair
lining up butter cookies like delectable soldiers.

On the other, my father and the men
kneading batch after batch of lard and sugar
with their big, rough knuckles—
flour rising from their hands.

And on the wall above them,
where I wasn't supposed to see,
a calendar of topless women,
a different one every month,
each with breasts as fleshy as dough,
and skin as smooth as *Battatina's*.

I Think I Love You

After dinner when we'd clean up,
Janine would
cajole us into song and dance.

Our mother would try to resist,
clinging to soapy dish,
twitch forming on her face,
but Janine was much taller.

She'd pry my and Julie's hands away
from broom and dishcloth,
pulling us into
the space between table and stove.

She'd belt out *I Think I Love You*
marble eyes widening with each lyric,
cowlick swaying to the side—
and soon we were singing
I Think I Love You back.
Soon we were that family on TV—

all of us in ruffles,
all of us playing our part
mommy in a pageboy slapping her thigh to keep time,
Julie on keyboard with long, swaying hair,
me, with bangs and missing tooth and tambourine—

I'm afraid that I'm not sure of
a love that there's no cure for.

As the years went on, the songs changed,
Elton, Commodores, Springsteen.
Our baby sister, Nellie, was born,
came with her own moves.

Janine remained the one
in that kitchen on 84th Street,
that smelled of garlic and Joy,
the one who pulled the music out of us,
helped us make our own song.

Destiny

Brown eyes and brown curly hair,
uniform tie
that made him look like a little man.
He sat behind me in class,
touched my hair
like he wanted something of me to hold onto.

When he transferred in sixth grade,
I was crushed,
though he asked me to one of his dances,
rang my bell while his father waited in the car.
I remember the inside of his prep school,
the smell of leather-bound books
the dark, mild night,
then nothing for years.
I thought I might see him at my 8th grade prom,
held at his uncle's catering hall,
fantasized him asking me to dance,
me in white eyelet and wrist corsage.
He wasn't there.

Two years later
he finally asked me out—
the summer I brought him back a t-shirt from
the Bahamas,
the summer that Sting played over and over in my head.
Imagining him
watching every move I made,
which I thought meant love,

which frightened me.

I remember my first kiss, our first kiss,
the two of us sitting on my front stoop,
the neighbor across the street mowing the lawn,
the smell of green and James' tongue just a little in my mouth.
I remember dreaming of taffeta wedding dresses
and the nervous butterflies.
I remember telling my sister *If I don't marry James,*
I'm becoming a nun.

Before the end of summer, he broke up with me,
leaned on the air conditioner in our yard
told me he was too busy.
I knew what that meant,
still, I invited him to my Sweet 16
the following year.

He said he couldn't come, dropped off a gift for me
while I was at Mass.
Gucci perfume and a card that read
I'll always love you and remember your smile.
The past may be hard to forget, but who knows
what the future may hold?

Six Years Apart

In the picture, my sister and me
on the mustard-colored couch.
I'm two, she's eight. She in a
red, knee-length dress,
her hair in an adorable pixie,
and me in a blue and white dress,
my hair light brown curls,
the side of my hand in my mouth.

She has her arm around me,
and we're sitting close, smiling,
unlike the picture from my baptism—
my godmother holding me
above the enormous marble font,
family encircling us,
little Julie, in her flair coat and bonnet,
with face that says,
Why did you have to come?

Many years later when I try to explain
the distance I feel with her
to an old friend, he asks,
"Did you ever consider you stole her paradise?"

If so, it's only half the story.
In my twenties and thirties,
I held a grudge like a pointed finger.

Growing up, I was always trying to close
the six-year gap, while she was looking
for someone to run her errands.
The summer I turned twelve
and wasn't allowed to shave, she prodded,
"What's with the thick knee socks in 90 degree heat?"

This the sister who years later
left "You Got a Friend" on my voicemail
and sweet homegrown tomatoes on my doorstep,
who threw me a surprise 25th
and hosted so many others.

This the sister who's read all my poems twice,
and shared them,
who tells me how proud of me she is.

The sister who put her arm around me
that winter I despaired,
who sat as close to me on my couch
as she did that day when were
still little girls in bright dresses with bright eyes,
no space between us.

December 8

Our mother always waited until
the Immaculate Conception,
before she decorated.

She pulled out
garland and lights
and the gold, antique fruit,

danced the Christmas tree
into its red-bowl stand.

She sprayed the windows
with snow
and belted
Christmas Card to You
with my sisters and me.

She tied the mistletoe
and spread the tablecloths,
hand made ornaments she hung with satin string.

Outside she wrapped lights
around both sides of our house,
fixed colored bulbs into the Holy Family
except for Jesus dim in His hay.

She baked and shopped, wrapped and cooked,
poured herself out.

In other homes, Christmas started
the day after Thanksgiving,
but we waited.

How could the Savior of the world be born
without His mother,

how could I have learned
to cherish my faith
without mine?

Favorite Toys

Fisher Price milk bottles
with alluringly bright colored caps,
set of six in yellow tray with handle.

Wooden dollhouse that Santa brought,
catty cornered beneath the small square window
in our basement next to Mom's sewing machine.

The miniature furniture I was allowed
to select one piece at a time—the tiny pedestal sink
whose porcelain shone like a gleaming eye.

The Big Wheel with the royal blue trunk
that taught me the freedom of tires and speed,
how to go fast, how to fly.

The Darci barbie-doll
with the side ponytail I *adored*
whose heart could not be broken.

The softball mitt
that got better with age,
that cushioned the blows.

When I played Perfection,
I loved beating the sixty seconds,
matching the small geometric shapes into the right spot
before time ran out.

There was no dark side to Life
—with its roulette wheel in the middle
that told me how many steps to advance
which direction to go in—
where the only bad thing that could happen
is that I wound up in last place.

In Praise of Irises

Named after the Greek goddess
who carried messages from heaven to earth
on the arc of a rainbow,
their long stems flourished in our yard,
lining the path to our stoop and front door.

Each May they seemed to spring suddenly.
One day none,
the next a whole chorus
of violet singing
as we came and went,
as we posed for graduations, sacraments.

So many of them, my mother
cut and blanketed them like babies
for the Blessed Mother.

They kept me company as I roller-skated,
as I watched my older sisters go off
to do things I wasn't allowed to do,
as I played hide and seek with my younger.

This spring so many decades later,
I'm surprised again
when I see the first one—
so luxurious I have to get
down on the ground
to confirm it's not velvet
sprung from the earth.

Thirteen

Feeling pretty special
in white and pink summer outfit,
barrette with streaming ribbon

flanked by girls
I liked, girls I trusted.

Jennifer, rebel
Cetta, straight arrow
Christine, artist
RoseMary, mother hen,
Donna, friend from vacation.

Girls playing Twister
in a basement,
dancing on linoleum,
eating sandwiches and drinking root beer,
balloons clinging to drop ceiling.

When it came time to sing,
they circled me and the cake,

smiled widely for the camera,
all of us with plump complexions
and clear eyes.

At midnight, we opened
the vinyl black couch
into queen sleeper,

surrounded it with sleeping bags,
put on pjs
but still weren't ready for bed.

All these years later,
I've only stayed in touch
with two, the rest
disappearing into their lives.

I like to think I carry
all of them with me, the gifts they brought,

this circle of girls
on the verge of our lives.

Pointer Sisters

We never made it to the concert
that summer I turned fifteen,
my older sisters' car
steaming ribbons of fumes on the Brooklyn Gowanus
as we sat with hazards waiting to be towed.

Until then I'd only moved to music
that came from radio or records,
only went out with my older sisters on a holiday.
I always wanted to belong to them
the way they belonged to each other,
always looked for them in a crowd
at my games and awards nights
and that summer in the Catskills
when I was nine and sang
"I Write the Songs" in the talent show.

I wore denim gauchos and a silky, man-tailored blouse,
my face bright red from six-hour days in the pool
with no sunblock. My mother, Aunt Rose
and two-year-old Nellie rooting for me,
but it was the two teenage girls
in Jordache and lipstick
who were off in the woods smoking with the lifeguard
who I wanted to see me singing my heart out
in that smoky lounge at nine years old,
who I wanted to see me when the emcee
with his thick black moustache and corduroy blazer
called me up, awarded me first prize,

those girls I wanted to sing with now.

What I Remember About the Dress

Royal blue taffeta,
strapless on a slant
fitted, then full like Belle's.

I posed on the front lawn
in May with my date
then again in October

beside my sister in her wedding gown
our heads titled toward each other
in our mother's living room,
then next to her on the altar
in the same basilica all the women
in my family married in.

Gathering her train,
fixing her veil
signing my name in the registry
after she and my brother-in-law exchanged vows.
I *did* feel honored:
barely eighteen still with a lisp,
this sister I'd been trying to
catch up to all my life,
how chubby and insecure I felt next to her,
until this day, until now,

my hair coaxed into smooth sleek waves,
my eyes almost as blue as the dress,

the dress that reminds me that she chose me
and they chose each other,
that even though decades pass,
they close gaps—
even though love can hurt,
it also heals,
can last no matter what.

Bridge

Driving on the Belt Parkway
on a brisk, winter night,
the Verrazano ascends
from Bay Ridge, a perfect arch
over the Narrows.

Gracing the barges
and potholes below,
the cables fall
like a necklace of white gold
stretching between towers
that rise from the water
like a woman's shoulders.
Each light's a diamond strung
between the forts—Hamilton and Wadsworth,
but inside its mortar,
men fell to a different death.

It appears as the parkway bends west
from the place of my childhood—
Nellie Bly Amusement Park—
when thrill spun from a wide spool of tickets,
and being a few yards above ground
was enough to soar.

I peer up at lights even more intense
against the season's frigid sky,
lean closer to the windshield
like trying to read a highway sign

when almost past it. This is my exit—
the place this Bridge exacts for me
where origin, like beams,
sustains the crossing.

Manhattan Beach

Aunt Anna sailed the Belt Parkway
in her and Uncle Mimi's
big brown boat of a Cadillac,
then turned off
Coney Island Ave onto West End,

my older sisters and cousins
laughing so hard they snorted,
our mothers yelling, "Cut it out!"
over Carole King singing
"I Feel the Earth Move"
as I sat squished on the hump in the backseat.

I remember tearing off my cover up,
running for the water,
swimming from 9 – 5 like it was a career
except when I got called out.
I'd insist I wasn't hungry or cold
my lips as blue as a bruise,
the adults covering me in terry cloth,
handing me a tuna sandwich
they pulled from the colorful insulated bag.

I remember my navy blue and green one piece
and Aunt Rose combing the ocean out of my hair

I remember the kissing teenagers
and the portable barbecues under the boardwalk

the wide-open space and the sea of people.

There was no way twelve of us fit in one car—
nine kids, three adults.
No way our lunches fit in one cooler.
No way that one song played
all the way from Dyker Heights to Manhattan Beach.
Yet, that's what I remember,
this and how my mother and aunts taught us
to stay together,
how to spread out our blankets

and live.

In Gratitude

To Maria Mazziotti Gillan and Ed Hack, writing-parents, who have shown me how to go to the page with courage and heart and have helped foster my writing life; to Ed, for truly helping this collection, and all my writing, come to the best possible light.

To everyone at Bordighera Press for their continued faith in my work—Anthony Tamburri, Fred Gardaphé, Paolo Giordano, and Nic Grosso for his kind professionalism and keen eye. It's a privilege.

To my poet-friends in our monthly workshop—LMF, ED, RN and JP—for their invaluable feedback on a handful of poems in this collection.

To all the gifted poets and writers who help hold me up.

And, especially, to all the people who live in my poems for helping me . . . become.

In loving and cherished memory of Aunt "Rose" and Zia Rita.

Acknowledgements

Grateful acknowledgements to the editors of the following journals in which these poems first appear:

"Admissions" and "Mass in Rochester," *Paterson Literary Review,* 2025

"Arizona," WAYE, Winter 2025

"*Battatina,*" *Italian Americana*, Winter 2023

"*Call the Midwife,*" *I-70 Review,* September 2024

"Driving North on 287," *Exit 13*, Issue 30 Fall 2025

"Faith Is," *Offerings, A Spiritual Poetry Anthology,* 2022

"First Bedroom," *Ovunque Siamo*, Summer 2025

"I Used to Listen to the Saddest Love Song," *Tiferet*, Autumn/ Winter 2019

"If We Still Lived Where I Was Born," *New York Quarterly*, 68.1 August 2022

"*La Vita e Bella,*" *Voices in Italian Americana*, 13.1 Spring 2023

"Last Supper I and II," *Vita Poetica*, Winter 2022

"Manhattan Beach," *Ovunque Siamo*, Volume 1, Issue 3 2021

"My Parents Long Ago," *Lips*, 2024

"Sicily in June," *Paterson Literary Review*, 2023

"Sister of Charity," *Presence: A Journal of Catholic Poetry*, 2024

"Six Years Apart," *Paterson Literary Review,* 2024

"Sunday," *Paterson Literary Review,* 2022

"Uncle Mimi," *Celebrating Calabria: Writing Heritage and Memory,* 2020 Rubbettino Editore

About the Author

MARIA GIURA is also the author of *Celibate: A Memoir*, which won a 1ˢᵗ place Independent Press Award, and *What My Father Taught Me*. An Academy of American Poets winner, Giura has been published in several journals including *New York Quarterly, Prime Number, I-70, Liguorian, Presence, Midstory, PLR, Italian Americana and Voices in Italian Americana*. She's taught at multiple universities including Binghamton University where she received her PhD in English and currently teaches writing workshops for Casa Belvedere Cultural Foundation.

VIA Folios

A refereed book series dedicated to the culture of Italians and Italian Americans.

MARK CIABATTARI. *Dreams of An Imaginary New Yorker Named Rizzoli.*
   Vol. 146. Novel.
LAURETTE FOLK. *The End of Aphrodite.* Vol. 145. Novel.
ANNA CITRINO. *A Space Between.* Vol. 144. Poetry
MARIA FAMÀ. *The Good for the Good.* Vol. 143. Poetry.
ROSEMARY CAPPELLO. *Wonderful Disaster.* Vol. 142. Poetry.
B. AMORE. *Journeys on the Wheel.* Vol. 141. Poetry.
ALDO PALAZZESCHI. *The Manifestos of Aldo Palazzeschi.* Vol 140. Literature.
ROSS TALARICO. *The Reckoning.* Vol 139. Poetry.
MICHELLE REALE. *Season of Subtraction.* Vol 138. Poetry.
MARISA FRASCA. *Wild Fennel.* Vol 137. Poetry.
RITA ESPOSITO WATSON. *Italian Kisses.* Vol. 136. Memoir.
SARA FRUNER. *Bitter Bites from Sugar Hills.* Vol. 135. Poetry.
KATHY CURTO. *Not for Nothing.* Vol. 134. Memoir.
JENNIFER MARTELLI. *My Tarantella.* Vol. 133. Poetry.
MARIA TERRONE. *At Home in the New World.* Vol. 132. Essays.
GIL FAGIANI. *Missing Madonnas.* Vol. 131. Poetry.
LEWIS TURCO. *The Sonnetarium.* Vol. 130. Poetry.
JOE AMATO. *Samuel Taylor's Hollywood Adventure.* Vol. 129. Novel.
BEA TUSIANI. *Con Amore.* Vol. 128. Memoir.
MARIA GIURA. *What My Father Taught Me.* Vol. 127. Poetry.
STANISLAO PUGLIESE. *A Century of Sinatra.* Vol. 126. Popular Culture.
TONY ARDIZZONE. *The Arab's Ox.* Vol. 125. Novel.
PHYLLIS CAPELLO. *Packs Small Plays Big.* Vol. 124. Literature.
FRED GARDAPHÉ. *Read 'em and Reap.* Vol. 123. Criticism.
JOSEPH A. AMATO. *Diagnostics.* Vol 122. Literature.
DENNIS BARONE. *Second Thoughts.* Vol 121. Poetry.
OLIVIA K. CERRONE. *The Hunger Saint.* Vol 120. Novella.
GARIBLADI M. LAPOLLA. *Miss Rollins in Love.* Vol 119. Novel.
JOSEPH TUSIANI. *A Clarion Call.* Vol 118. Poetry.
JOSEPH A. AMATO. *My Three Sicilies.* Vol 117. Poetry & Prose.
MARGHERITA COSTA. *Voice of a Virtuosa and Coutesan.* Vol 116. Poetry.
NICOLE SANTALUCIA. *Because I Did Not Die.* Vol 115. Poetry.
MARK CIABATTARI. *Preludes to History.* Vol 114. Poetry.
HELEN BAROLINI. *Visits.* Vol 113. Novel.
ERNESTO LIVORNI. *The Fathers' America.* Vol 112. Poetry.
MARIO B. MIGNONE. *The Story of My People.* Vol 111. Non-fiction.
GEORGE GUIDA. *The Sleeping Gulf.* Vol 110. Poetry.
JOEY NICOLETTI. *Reverse Graffiti.* Vol 109. Poetry.
GIOSE RIMANELLI. *Il mestiere del furbo.* Vol 108. Criticism.
LEWIS TURCO. *The Hero Enkidu.* Vol 107. Poetry.
AL TACCONELLI. *Perhaps Fly.* Vol 106. Poetry.
RACHEL GUIDO DEVRIES. *A Woman Unknown in Her Bones.* Vol 105. Poetry.
BERNARD BRUNO. *A Tear and a Tear in My Heart.* Vol 104. Non-fiction.
FELIX STEFANILE. *Songs of the Sparrow.* Vol 103. Poetry.
FRANK POLIZZI. *A New Life with Bianca.* Vol 102. Poetry.

GIL FAGIANI. *Stone Walls*. Vol 101. Poetry.

LOUISE DESALVO. *Casting Off*. Vol 100. Fiction.

MARY JO BONA. *I Stop Waiting for You*. Vol 99. Poetry.

RACHEL GUIDO DEVRIES. *Stati zitt, Josie*. Vol 98. Children's Literature. $8

GRACE CAVALIERI. *The Mandate of Heaven*. Vol 97. Poetry.

MARISA FRASCA. *Via incanto*. Vol 96. Poetry.

DOUGLAS GLADSTONE. *Carving a Niche for Himself*. Vol 95. History.

MARIA TERRONE. *Eye to Eye*. Vol 94. Poetry.

CONSTANCE SANCETTA. *Here in Cerchio*. Vol 93. Local History.

MARIA MAZZIOTTI GILLAN. *Ancestors' Song*. Vol 92. Poetry.

MICHAEL PARENTI. *Waiting for Yesterday: Pages from a Street Kid's Life*. Vol 90. Memoir.

ANNIE LANZILLOTTO. *Schistsong*. Vol 89. Poetry.

EMANUEL DI PASQUALE. *Love Lines*. Vol 88. Poetry.

CAROSONE & LOGIUDICE. *Our Naked Lives*. Vol 87. Essays.

JAMES PERICONI. *Strangers in a Strange Land: A Survey of Italian-Language American Books*.Vol 86. Book History.

DANIELA GIOSEFFI. *Escaping La Vita Della Cucina*. Vol 85. Essays.

MARIA FAMÀ. *Mystics in the Family*. Vol 84. Poetry.

ROSSANA DEL ZIO. *From Bread and Tomatoes to Zuppa di Pesce "Ciambotto"*. Vol. 83. Memoir.

LORENZO DELBOCA. *Polentoni*. Vol 82. Italian Studies.

SAMUEL GHELLI. *A Reference Grammar*. Vol 81. Italian Language.

ROSS TALARICO. *Sled Run*. Vol 80. Fiction.

FRED MISURELLA. *Only Sons*. Vol 79. Fiction.

FRANK LENTRICCHIA. *The Portable Lentricchia*. Vol 78. Fiction.

RICHARD VETERE. *The Other Colors in a Snow Storm*. Vol 77. Poetry.

GARIBALDI LAPOLLA. *Fire in the Flesh*. Vol 76 Fiction & Criticism.

GEORGE GUIDA. *The Pope Stories*. Vol 75 Prose.

ROBERT VISCUSI. *Ellis Island*. Vol 74. Poetry.

ELENA GIANINI BELOTTI. *The Bitter Taste of Strangers Bread*. Vol 73. Fiction.

PINO APRILE. *Terroni*. Vol 72. Italian Studies.

EMANUEL DI PASQUALE. *Harvest*. Vol 71. Poetry.

ROBERT ZWEIG. *Return to Naples*. Vol 70. Memoir.

AIROS & CAPPELLI. *Guido*. Vol 69. Italian/American Studies.

FRED GARDAPHÉ. *Moustache Pete is Dead! Long Live Moustache Pete!*. Vol 67. Literature/Oral History.

PAOLO RUFFILLI. *Dark Room/Camera oscura*. Vol 66. Poetry.

HELEN BAROLINI. *Crossing the Alps*. Vol 65. Fiction.

COSMO FERRARA. *Profiles of Italian Americans*. Vol 64. Italian Americana.

GIL FAGIANI. *Chianti in Connecticut*. Vol 63. Poetry.

BASSETTI & D'ACQUINO. *Italic Lessons*. Vol 62. Italian/American Studies.

CAVALIERI & PASCARELLI, Eds. *The Poet's Cookbook*. Vol 61. Poetry/Recipes.

EMANUEL DI PASQUALE. *Siciliana*. Vol 60. Poetry.

NATALIA COSTA, Ed. *Bufalini*. Vol 59. Poetry.

RICHARD VETERE. *Baroque*. Vol 58. Fiction.

www.ingramcontent.com/pod-product-compliance
Lightning Source LLC
Chambersburg PA
CBHW020208090426

42734CB00008B/982